Lies, Deception and Coercions

Harassed by the Orono PD

By William John Crandall

I dedicate this book to all those who are victims of the lawlessness of the Orono Police Department, the illegal acts committed against an individual through illegal searches and seizures to warrantless entrance to your domicile. I dedicate this book also to those who are deceptively tricked into going to hospitals under false pretenses and being falsely committed on holidays to sustain weekends of miserable torment. Furthermore, I dedicate this book to those who are medically compromised by the ignorance of the law enforcement against their personal safety. I also dedicate this book to my loving wife who had to tolerate the ignorance of law enforcement individuals who falsely committed me to a hospital against physician's recommendations.

Growing up New England

I grew up in North Stonington Connecticut living on, get this Sleepy Hollow Road. The house was located between the Davis's and the Anderson's less than a quarter of a mile down street from an old-fashioned Civil War graveyard. The schoolhouse was centrally

located in the town square along with the churches in the town.

North Stonington was a wooded combination of a farmland environment.

The New England winters could be very grueling such as the blizzard of 1978 where we were forced to heat the house by fireplace, eat dinners by candlelight, use the fireplace for cooking and hauling water a quarter mile from the brook.

I remember before dad left mom our family Thanksgiving dinners and Christmas suppers were spent together as a family unit.

As a youth my family always gave me cap guns and to play cowboys and Indians with Eric Davis next door.

Being a child in a rural Connecticut farm community, I had an extreme love for horses being that I was not allowed to have one of my own. I would cut down trees and tie ropes to them to make a fictionalized halter to the tree stumps pretending to be my actual horse.

I did have my first experience with horses at my first job with the Bishop's at the end of the street and our annual trip to Six Gun City New Hampshire.

Growing up in rural North Stonington, Connecticut did have his it's trials and tribulations especially when being retained for one year in the kindergarten because I was too rambunctious to sit still all day in class.

I guess I have always had the heart of a great outdoorsman and environmentalist always spending every free moment outside or in the woods. I am a very trusting person, kind of an animal whisperer because animals trust me enough to come up to me in the woods.

My first job at the age of 10 was mucking out stalls, raking leaves splitting wood, and helping the Bishop's out around the farm.

I learned my farming techniques from the Anderson's where I learned to slaughter pigs and cows and butcher them for meat.

Farming was a big to do every planting season and the harvest in the fall. My formative years were spent with outdoor activities such as the recreational departments youth football, youth basketball, and Little League baseball.

I was really good at everything I did because of the fact I have a 185 IQ, a photographic memory, and the ability to read and comprehend both sides of a book at the same time. Every fall when school began, we would make our annual trip to the B.F. Clyde Cider Mill which was planned annually and was the highlight on my school year.

In the fall before Dad left Mom, we always had our annual visits to the Mohawk Trail in Massachusetts where we visited all the Native American gift shops and the annual New England Pow-Wow held each year.

Winters were great growing up in New England , I would attend weekly meetings as a Cub scout by night and have our daily snowball fight in the sun sparkled snow sometimes, we even went ice skating and

played ice hockey.

We as youths valued our free time in the environment unlike the youth of today, we actually had a great respect for mother nature. The American youth of today has gotten fat and lazy playing games inside where I was actually born to the woods. I can always know where I am in the woods because my body is a geo-locating entity born to the environment, I never come out farther than 10 ft. from my destination location. I use a paper map and compass for triangulation rather than a GPS but really, they are moot and unnecessary because I always end up in the same spot I started.

I always tested well far above the average individual never scoring a test below a hundred.

Every fall I would attend the local School pep rally where they had a huge bonfire, served

cider and donuts, and had Mr Pizza's pizza by the slice. While everyone enjoy the extravaganza well into the night we all made friends and made family remained comfortable throughout the situation.

I attended the North Stonington elementary School until I graduated and moved on to Wheeler Junior high School where I enjoyed learning the Sciences from Mr. Kerr who

actually had a stuffed Cobra as a class exhibit.

My sister Mary was a basketball team player, my sister Kim was an artist who painted pictures, my mom was an ex-registered nurse and my dad was a business owner in construction and hazardous waste hauling. Dad never attended any of my after-school functions but like clockwork mom always was there in the audience cheering me on.

If I was not in the woods at home, I spent most of my time doing chores for Grandma Crandall because I was the only one of the 19 grandchildren who would not even lift a finger to help her.

Growing up in rural North Stonington Connecticut and basically owning Stonington and Mystic my family we're basically involved in some way in every day-to-day operations of the town. Our annual Apple fest took place every year especially during the harvest season and the annual blessing of the

fleet took place during the summer where they did boat parades up the harbor.

Mystic itself historically is the whaling capital of the world with the famous ship the Captain Morgan as part of its fleet. I also lived 10 miles from the United States naval submarine base in Groton Connecticut and 5 mi from the beaches of Misquamicut in Rhode Island I spent my time as a youth working for a causes that were better for the environment.

Journey to Adulthood

I began my journey into adulthood when, I graduated from elementary school and the

Cub Scouts to enter into junior high school and the local Boy Scout unit.

I took up every skills badge that the boy scouts had to offer and became proficient in archery obtaining the golden archer award. One of my friends was a Native American so I learned all my survival training and how to survive off the land through my Native

American friends as well as learning their arts and crafts

with their uniqueness of creativity and design of their arts and crafts.

Dad had finally showed back up in the picture and I was immediately groomed to take over operations of the town of Pawcatuck, Connecticut hazardous waste program.

I also started to learn the new career of Welding and Fabrication by Uncle Fred who worked as a shipbuilder for General Dynamics Electric Boat in Groton, Connecticut.

In the winters we would do snow removal for the area schools and the local nuclear facility, where I obtained my top-secret clearance because I had to have access to the lower base in Groton, Connecticut where the nuclear submarines were docked.

I attended all my classes and kept my nose in the books, kind of a bookworm fueling my 185 IQ and photographic memory with more education that my brain could possibly handle.

Mom had us active within the Catholic Church going every Sunday and while attending I served as an altar boy. Dad was Baptist and Mom a maternal Catholic we were raised as Catholic in the eyes of God.

However, my belief in God also extended through invitation to attend nights at the local

Baptist Church studying Bible verse right next door. I graduated from AWANA's winning the award for the most books memorized.

I would spend hot summer days up street at Chad Vandale's swimming in his swimming pool in his back yard.

I even helped the Slavic's deliver newspapers until one day the Wilkinson's dog followed us into the streets and was hit by a speeding car and killed by a driver who never even

stopped.

During the hot summer months, I would also spend some days with Travis Santos and his mom clam digging and swimming in the ocean on Mason's Island in Mystic, Connecticut next to the seminary.

We always at Christmas time would attend the local annual fire department Christmas party where they served dinner, had a raffle and presented children with Christmas gifts.

I was becoming more self sufficient through my annual survival training as a boy scout attending the annual Klondike at Patchaug State forest.

The Klondike involved gathering water, chopping wood, pan-mining, rope bridge building and gathering food available in the winter. I have always excelled at everything that I do sitting back and observing your fatal flaw to best place my position of attack. I do survival training for all adverse circumstances hot or cold, being an environmentalist I really don't need human beings at all.

    I have learned through experience with the Orono, Maine Police Department that

ignorance of the law by those meant to protect us is not only obtrusive and in

violation of the Fourth Amendment it is also a ACLU matter. I have lived my life alone because I lay back and observe because strategically advancing without a plan can get your flank over run and your ranks decimated.

I worked long and hard for the family and during the summer we would wind the day down by rewarding ourselves with a night out at the Misquamicut beach arcade extravaganza .

Every Thanksgiving and Christmas mom would get in and fix us a feast for us to eat

while we watched the local sports games and annual holiday parade.

We raised most of our own produce and what we did not raise my dad's client s would barter to pay for their bills.

I spent the summer with Mom at Grandma's and Grandpas in Bonita Springs, Florida. The Crandall's have always been financially safe but Grandpa's family owns the largest subsidized farming operation in Kentucky, known as the Hagman farm. I learned at an early age from my family experience that true success comes when you can legally squash the bugs. Revenge is not acceptable but sometimes retribution from a wrong is a dish best served cold.

The school year was dragging on, it was my eighth grade year and opportunity stirred inside me and I took the entrance exam into Ella Grasso Southeastern Technical High School and passed with a 100% so now I would be transferred to school in Groton Connecticut. I spent the summer of 1984 working for Dad and the North Stonington fairgrounds. We enjoyed every year the fair coming around the rides, the livestock, the pulls, and the sausage sandwich and even the fried blooming onions as well as a tasty dough boy. I spent my time haying the fields which truly distinguishes the boys from the men, something that the Orono, Maine police department could ever handle. The annual blessing is the fleet and the artistic splendor of the art festival spikes intrigue and enthusiasm in the coldest of hearts. The blessing the of fleet was a family event bringing a closeness and sense of security of heart.

High School Jungle

In 1984 I entered my journey at Ella Grasso Southeastern Technical High School to work towards a career in Automotive Technician Technology My first car that I bought was a brand new Ford Mustang equipped with a 4 speed Hurst transmission and speed shifter.. The Ford Mustang was the place that I lost my virginity on a back woods road in the country. I always was a team player and loved playing team sports in 1984 I joined the rifle club at Southeastern Technical High School officiated by the Rocketto brothers who taught the physics classes.

The first year of technical school was trial and error by taking one week of each class to better see what your career options could be. I chose Automotive Technician and Service Writing for my career options.

I begin each day at sun up to sundown attending my classes and even my shop

keeping in mind school is just not just away a hop, because I skip to the moment and I then un-tool from the hip. I took all my classes every day even plowing snow to earn extra money while working for family which did not have its perks because I ended up with the crappiest of works.

Mom was angry and even upset when I drove up in my friend's Corvette. Mom was against my driver's education class because she was afraid it would put me on my death bed. She caved into my driver's education class with a stipulation.

Mom said if I got my license I would have to pay my own gas and car maintenance. I took my driver's examination on December 18,

1985 at the New, London branch of the Connecticut Department of Motor Vehicles making it a day very well spent I passed my examination with 100 percent, now I was a licensed driver wow it was perfect and decent

I made the National Honor Society each quarter, being a grill cook at McDonald's to a stationary sorter.

I would spend some of my time at the farm mucking the stall when duties a must farm work is your call. I took everything from culinary arts to automotive class with my final high school education being Automotive Technician Training.

I worked for National Tire senior year strung out but hell bent on fire to have such a job and career but never once touching a drug or a beer. The winter of 1987 was a dangerous and icy one, I slated my 1985 Ford Mustang off the road and in a blink of an eye my mustang was gone.

Damage being done and the accident not being helped the Mustang was a total mess I however, was safe never the less. My second vehicle was the family business Stepside Chevy pickup truck because I was family the truck didn't cost me a buck.

The truck was mine for work and school it was more than just pleasure but a working tool. I plowed snow for the nuclear weapons plant when it snowed cleaning out the zones never a stalled moment always on the go. Time had passed Thanksgiving and Christmas gone snow melt to the birth of a new born fawn.

Graduation day came so fast it was time for school's final blast. The prom was basically a place to enjoy and say goodbye because a whole new era was beginning, one could not deny. My graduation was not the end, God only knew what was around the bend.

I spent the summer working for family doing lot developments which this new world experience only enlightened me. I had a choice and a decision to choose no matter what direction I could not lose in.

After graduation I worked for the family for a brief period of time working construction earning extra money to attend Heavy

Equipment Technician at Wyoming Technical Institute in Laramie, .Wyoming

The summer passed excavating and developing residential homes ground up construction to finished product landscape architecture. I took my final position at the North Stonington, Connecticut for July 1988. Time passed being October 21, 1988, I made

my journey to Laramie, Wyoming for my Heavy Equipment Technician training.

Unveiling the Cowboy Within

I flew out to Laramie, Wyoming on October 21, 1988 to attend the Wyoming Technical Institute training program for Heavy Equipment Technician Training. I walked off the plane in Denver, Colorado, with a 6-hour layover which I spent at the Denver Museum of Natural History.

After my visit to the Museum I flew out of Denver, Colorado to finish the journey to Laramie, Wyoming landing in good old Laramie, Wyoming at 5:30 PM MST and immediately checking in at the Laramie Wyoming Holiday Inn.

I was really jet lagged so I got some takeout from the hotel restaurant and ate in my room and turning in early settling down to sleep at around 9:00 PM MST. The following day I ate breakfast at the Chuck-wagon restaurant and then made my way over to Wyoming Technical Institute.

I checked in with the college at Wyoming Technical Institute and picked up my belongings and immediately went to residential housing at the college dormitory.

I was settled and unpacked and headed back to the hotel where I went across the street and got my Chili lunch with Cheddar cheese, onion, and hot buttered corn bread at the Chuck-wagon restaurant, which has a chili by far has no competition by any other.

I began training Monday October 24, 1988 in my first phase the Engine's phase learning all about Caterpillar, Detroit Diesel, and Cummins Engines.

I would spend weekend nights at the local Bowl-arama bowling alley spending time with Cheyenne and Shawnee playing moonlight bowling into the wee hours of the morning.

My breakfast I spent at the corner truck stop which was located on the corner of the road to the dormitory and just one quarter mile from I-80 cross country interstate highway. I would get my usual bacon and cheese omelette and home fries as well as a hot buttered biscuit.

The feeling of home sickness was strong until I met Patrick Whitman and his wife Lisa and son Tyrel for whom would take me to their ranch on the weekends to get away from school.

Patrick Whitman taught me to ranch and to pro-rope turning me into a true hearted cowboy. Patrick and I were preparing for the

Calgary Stampede in Calgary, Alberta, Canada. The second phase of my training at Wyoming Technical Institute was the Fluid Power and Electrical in the Heavy Equipment Technician program where I studied skid steer loader hydraulic systems, electric motors and wiring, and Allison transmissions as well as overall fluid power and electrical fundamentals.

I spent all my free time walking in the grueling cold too the truck stop and downtown to the University or the bowling alley. Patrick and Lisa would have me over every weekend to family dinner. Christmas came and time for Christmas break Patrick's family extended an invitation to spend Christmas with them at the ranch, however, I

already accepted the invitation to spend the holiday with my cousins in Denver, Colorado.

While in Colorado my cousins took me to Colorado Springs, Colorado to the Air Force Academy where I witnessed first hand the 5 plane fallen soldier formation, the Garden of the Gods, and Pikes Peak overlook.

I went again to the Denver Museum of Natural History and saw several IMAX theatre presentations one on the Raging Colorado River, one on the Polynesian Islands and one on the Birds of Prey about pterodactyls. I returned back to Wyoming Technical Institute to begin my third phase of training on Fuel Systems studying about fuel injectors, B-series Cummins and Bosch

injection pumps, and Caterpillar and Detroit Diesel fuel Systems.

Time was coming to a close in February 1989, I began my last 6 weeks cycle of training in Powertrains where I learned to rebuild manual transmissions rebuild differentials and fully diagnose and repair air braking systems.

As time grew nearer, mom made arrangements to come to my graduation with the cousins from Denver, Colorado to fly out and join me to witness my graduation. On April 1st, 1989, I graduated from Wyoming Technical Institute ranking 3rd in my class of 2000 students.

Mom and I spent two weeks with the cousins in Denver, Colorado before returning to Connecticut. Upon returning to the East Coast I decided to relocate to Lincoln, Maine to begin my show Appaloosas horse farm while working for the local concrete plant as a Heavy Equipment Technician.

I lived on Phinney Farm Rd and would trail ride around the lakes on the wooded trails as often as time permitted while practicing my pro-roping in hopes of some day competing in the Calgary Stampede in Calgary, Alberta, Canada with my pro-roping teammate Patrick Whitman.

Living in Stink in Lincoln

I returned to Lincoln, ME to start my horse farm Isfappaloosa Farms.

I started working for the concrete plant in Lincoln, ME in June of 1989. I bought my first horse Indian summer from the Okeson's in Woodville ME and I brought him home and built the barn all by myself on my new property in Lincoln, ME.

Times were a little tough in the beginning when I arrived to Lincoln, Maine because I originally had a hard time finding a job until I got the job at G.E. Goding and Sons concrete plant on route 2 in Lincoln. I started line dancing with Denim and Leather Dancers and began line dancing in Millinocket, run by Bobby Allen of Millinocket who was actually the one who drew me out of my shell and got me out to socialize with the public. We danced on the weekends at local dance halls such as the DAV Hall in Medway and the conference hall out in Milo, ME we also did demonstrations in Sherman, ME and Houlton ME on the weekends and we would do couples dancing classes on Sunday night in Medway. Line dancing was fun because it was a way to get out and express myself without making a fool of myself because the people that I went to class with were also under the same boat as I was.

My first real love was Janet Lawrence also of Lincoln, ME and do to unforeseen circumstances she broke off our engagement and to this day I have to believe that it was due to a medical situation because her mother

said that she couldn't explain why she did what she did.

I lived to hunt and fish during the proper seasons but the only thing that happened was I became an environmentalist and outdoorsman and I no longer hunt with a gun I hunt with a camera. I enjoy saltwater fishing and I would go whale watching on the weekends to express myself into the environment and make my point to correcting an injustice in this present and cruel world we live in.

The Godings every year would have a safety picnic day where we all went to Bar Harbor and spent the day enjoying the different attractions and then having a feast of a dinner at the Jasper's restaurant where we all had

BBQ ribs, a clambake and sweet corn on the cob.

 My friend Larry Grieco who taught me how to shoot with a handgun and get me proficient enough that I passed the sniper class grade qualifications in firearms proficiency. I have always been proficient in weapons from archery to firearms always passing everything with sniper grade qualifications.

I made an occasional trip to Connecticut when dad would volunteer me to go down and help move my sisters because they didn't want to pay for moving because they were too cheap to do it themselves and get it done. I would visit with mom occasionally while I was down there but once I was in Connecticut moving my sisters my father pretty much managed my time so I didn't have much time to spend with mom.

I rode a horse every day I rode in the in the woods on the wooded trails around the lakes down the street from where I lived on Phinney Farm Rd. in Lincoln. ME. My friends were Barber and Buster brown, Richard Tolman and Debbie Gendreau and of course Larry Greco and his wife Alicia as well as fellow friends from work Tim Hardy and Peter Dube. I owned, my own property in Mattawamkeag, ME and I used to go hunting every season during hunting season for Partridge and deer as well as applying for my moose permit but never receiving one to go on a moose hunt. I would spend my falls during leaf peeping season taking Sunday drives on the scenic road between Danforth and Houlton stopping for lunch at the restaurant overlooking the valley.

My second fiancée was Elizabeth Murphy who I hated to break things off with but due to the economic situation of working for the Goding's I couldn't support a family at the time of our engagement.

I took up welding engineering and steel fabrication as well as I went into my own custom furniture design business. I excelled at everything I did including Federal Motors carrier inspector and State of Maine vehicle Safety Inspector. Life was good I owned my own property management company and performed my own property maintenance. I continued to ride my horse and train for the

Calgary Stampede in Calgary, Alberta, Canada in hopes that Patrick Whitman and I could someday compete.

My third fiancée that I was involved with was Patty-Anne Robinson and her daughter who I became involved with was 6 months old in the beginning. I remember the first Christmas together Destiny Joy was too sick to even play with her toys and laid with her head over my heart that entire day.

I used to spoil Destiny Joy by buying her a Dalmatian ornament every day because that beautiful girl loved to collect them. I bought my first extended cab Chevy pickup truck in

1996 but crashed it into a tree and totaled it out. I replaced the pickup truck with a Pontiac Sunbird but also suffered a similar ill fate when I crashed under the back of a Tractor Trailer truck in 1999.

Patty-Anne Robinson called of a several years engagement when I was diagnosed with Bipolar Disorder in 1999. My medical issues related to degenerative back disease forced me into selling my farm and receiving medical attention from a specialist back surgeon in North Franklin, Connecticut.

Living Life with a Back Injury

I was forced into selling off the farm in Lincoln, ME due to an affliction in my back which requires a back specialist from Connecticut. I relocated to Connecticut on June 1st of the year in 1999 and began my grueling ordeal of 13 individual back surgeries.

I would attend our family outings on all the holidays such as the 4th of July pool party at

Uncle Frank's.

Mom was glad I decided to come to Connecticut to get the surgery procedure performed on my spine. I met my wife Alice

Kate Crandall while I was receiving the surgical procedures performed to correct years of damage through incorrectly lifting cylinder heads for heavy equipment engines and miscellaneous components.

I decided while I was receiving back surgery

that I would enroll at Three Rivers Community College to obtain my Civil and Environmental Engineering degree.

I spent 6 years obtaining my degrees in Civil

and Environmental Engineering

and I worked for the family part-time as a heavy equipment technician and welder fabricator. I worked alongside Uncle Fred until the pain from the sciatica got to great to

manage and I couldn't walk on or put any pressure on my left side.

I was walking one day and all of a sudden my left leg became paralyzed

and I couldn't get myself around my apartment so the physical therapy worker called me and ambulance

and sent me to Backus Hospital.

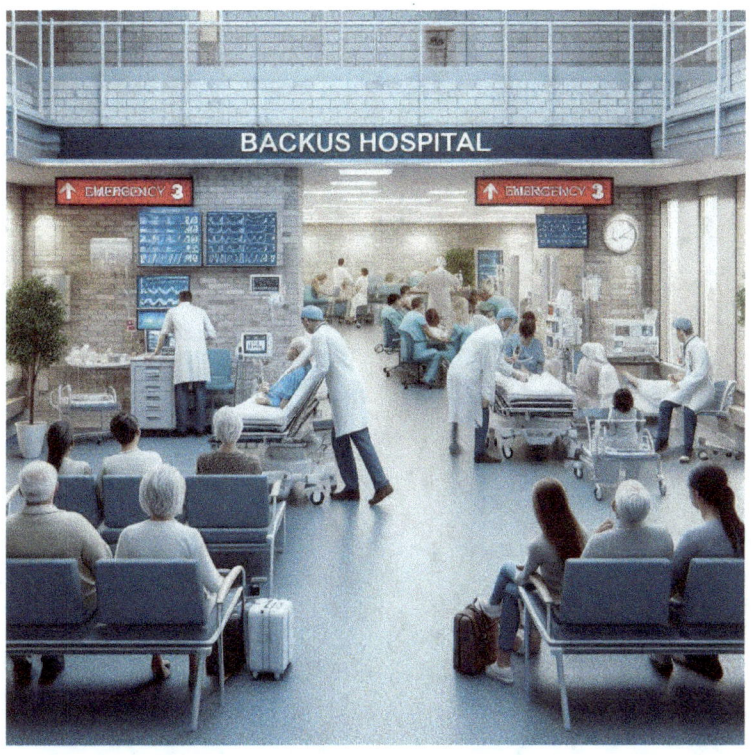

I got the word from my doctor that he could remove all my pain and endless operations by performing a total fusion of my spine so he turned me into the Terminator by putting 26 inches of steel in my spine.

I agreed to the operation which went well but after the surgery I blacked out and fell backwards on my back and caused total paralysis from the waist down.

Alice Kate Crandall was being shipped out on deployment the same time of my injury so she

was mid Atlantic when she received the message. Alice asked me what to do and I told her nothing because she surely could not jump ship and swim back.

I was in a wheelchair until December 14, 2020 when Dr. Halperin performed emergency surgery after I had blacked out and fallen breaking a piece of the steel off inside my body.

The second fusion of my spine gave me the ability to walk again. I then spent the grueling torment from my family for false committals to psychiatric facilities caused by my greedy

and manipulative family in Southeastern Connecticut.

The Return to the State of Maine

My return to me was plagued by the inconsiderate and consistent meddling by my family in Connecticut

having me investigated as a missing person in a person of concerns at the Portland ME Police Department on June 1st of 2021.

I was on my way home driving a U-Haul truck when I was ignorantly placed under arrest by the Portland Police Department

following a false report made by my sister Mary that I was a missing person and a person of concern in the state of Connecticut.

I lost all my personal belongings because while I was being detained by the Portland ME Police Department my U-Haul truck was gone through and all valuables stolen.

Like the current lawless police department of Orono, Maine the Portland, Maine police department subjected themselves to the same lawless acts

of Police intimidating and warrantless searches as well as unsubstantiated illegal searches and seizures violations of one's Fourth Amendment rights. I spent my first night back in the State of Maine under

incarceration by the Lawless police
department of the city of Portland, Maine

based on the fraudulent misguided and misrepresented accusations made by my nosey busy bodied family seeking greedy

motives while harassing my wife Alice Kate Crandall and myself all over the country.

I was cast into homelessness by the Portland, Maine Police department

when I was forced to sell the rest of the U-Haul truck contents and pay off my fines.

I was then forced to enter the Oxford Shelter

as a homeless client caused by my meddling family from Connecticut.

I was immediately taken from the Oxford Shelter to spend my days at the Days Inn in South Portland, Maine

where I served out the duration with the hotel until I relocated to Miami, Florida

to be together with my actively serving military wife Alice until she was redeployed to Camp Santiago, Puerto Rico.

Relocating to Miami

Relocating to Miami, Florida had challenges of its own, it began with the flight from Portland, Maine by the Northeast Angel Flight.non-profit organization setup for military

personnel in need of emergency services.

I flew into the Miami International Airport in Miami Springs, Florida.

I was shuttled to the Miami Springs Days Inn on 4767 Northwest 36th Street in Miami Springs, Florida.

9 I spent the entire month at the Days

Inn with Alice before she informed me that she was being deployed to Camp Santiago Puerto Rico.

I was not the happiest person on the planet because Alice had only been home one month from her last tour.

I was now left alone to fend for myself

in a location totally unfamiliar to me.

I was alright for the first month until I ran out of money and was ejected from the Days Inn Hotel

and forced to live at the Miami International Airport in Miami Springs, Florida as a homeless man

changing my clothes daily to avoid detection from the Miami-Dade police department. I spent 2 months changing out my clothes daily in the handicap stall of the men's room in the bathroom located by the Chili restaurant.

I was extremely successful in my coverage of my homelessness until one

evening I was severely sick and

discovered sleeping in the Latin American terminal at the Airport and cast out to collapse in the middle of the street in front of the homeless mission before I could seek entrance.

I was rushed by ambulance to the Jackson Memorial Hospital downtown Miami.

I spent two months getting back on my feet from severe malnutrition and malnourishment

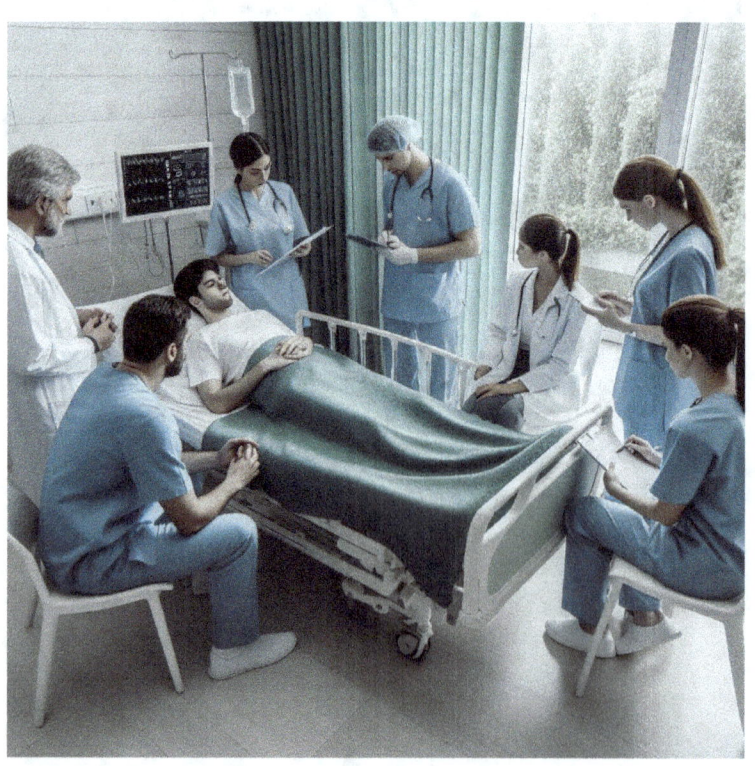

and another false committal at the hand of my meddling sister from Connecticut.

I recuperated until discharged to Joseph's assisted living facility where I spent the next 3 months regaining even more strength.

I flew out of Miami International Airport on February 5, 2022 bound for

Bangor, Maine on another Northeast Angel Flight. I arrived at the Concord Bus station in Bangor Maine after

spending the night at layover from the flight from Miami.

I was rushed from the bus station to Northern Lights Eastern Maine Medical Center with the COVID-19 virus and discharged because I was homeless to fend for myself on the streets of Bangor, Maine in one of the coldest winters on record

    Feeling for my situation Bruce and Donna from the Hope House Shelter offered me a place to stay while I recuperated from my affliction from the COVID-19 virus. I remained at the shelter until I obtained housing on the transition side of the shelter.

Living in Transitional Housing

Living in Bangor, Maine was quite a different experience than that of living in Lincoln, Maine.

The deceptive practices and the illegal acts witnessed at the Hope House Shelter was beyond belief such as the theft of my 2nd smartphone which the staff overlooked and did nothing to aid in retribution of the problem.

I was misrepresented by the Penobscot Community Health and Counseling into filing an unnecessary bankruptcy,

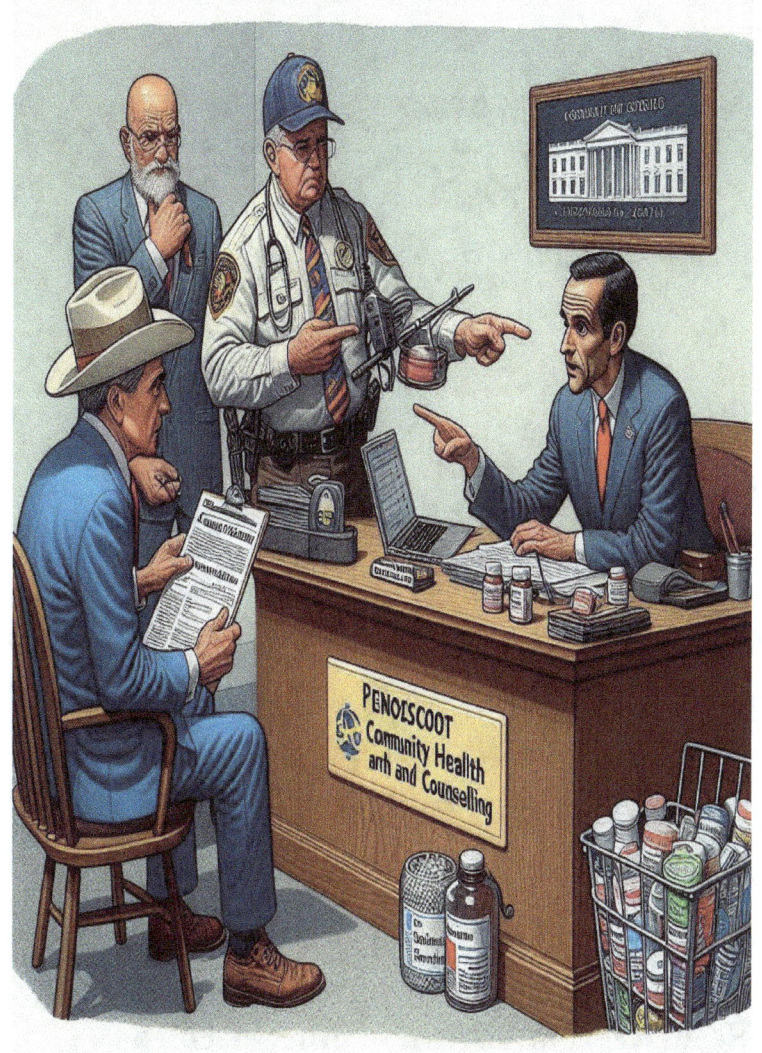

leading to the corruption inside the United States Government Social Security Administration office in Bangor, ME.

The United States Government Social Security Administration office decided because I filed the unnecessary bankruptcy that I was incapable of handling my own business affairs.

Graduation from Southern New Hampshire University gives me better qualifications than the bimbo that they assigned as a representative payee.

The representative payee Kennebec Behavioral Health is inadequate and incompetent because all my bills go unpaid.

The Social Security Administration illegally took my civil rights away but with the United

States Government who really gets held accountable for ACLU violations

The Hope House Shelter even prepared our meals 3 times a day sometimes even bringing snack food.

The transition housing was not so bad but the criminal elements still existed because my

phone was stolen, people were dealing drugs, people were being injured by baseball bats, knives and even gunfire.

I attended the Bangor Maine State Fair in the summer of 2023 and went to a couple of concerts to pass the time.

I even bought myself a drone so I could fly it around Bangor, Maine and investigate the sights around the area.

The only way I could get around because I don't own my own vehicle was to use public transportation, the city commuter bus.

The holidays at the shelter were boring because staff was minimal and nothing was done on the holiday.

I fought really hard to find my own

apartment so I could rid myself of the confinements of the transitional housing October 16, 2023 I finally moved out of transitional housing and into my apartment at the Glenridge Apartments in Orono, Maine.

I sold everything except my clothes the drone, knives, and even my second computer printer to Antonio so I would have as little as possible to carry to my new home in Orono, Maine.

The Law Breaking Orono, Maine Police Department

My journey began when I moved in the Glenridge Apartments in Orono, Maine on October 16, 2023. The inept Orono, Maine police department cannot effectively perform a thorough investigation because of they could they would find my family's baseless and unsubstantiated accusations are a fictitious and disrespectful attempt to gain my money and keep my wife Alice Kate Crandall from ever collecting a dime.

Personally my wife Alice Kate Crandall and myself are sick and tired of the lawless police department of Orono, Maine following through with the continued ongoing harassment associated with warrantless searches and illegal strip searches violating

my Fourth Amendment rights considering

my own personal investigation turned up a past history of the Orono, Maine Police Department violating the Codes of the ACLU.

I have become sickened by the lack of respect for the general public at the hand of the lawbreaking Orono, Maine Police Department. I found out that the Orono, Maine police department has broken several

laws not only against the Fourth Amendment but also the Eighth and Fourteenth Amendment as well.

The Lawbreaking police department of Orono, Maine also has violated such statutes as 42 U.S.C. 14141, 34 U.S.C. 12601.,

also the Orono Maine police department is in violation of the Civil Rights Act of 1871,and the Violent Crime Control and Law Enforcement Act of 1994.

The Lawbreaking police department of Orono, Maine has also violated federal 42 U.S.C. 1983 and Title 34-B sections 3803, 3862, and 3863

as well as Title 14 Chapter 747 section 8241 with issues also pertaining to violations against Title 17.

My journey began at Thanksgiving and Christmas of 2023 when my stupid family started with their bull crap of false accusations in an attempt to get me committed to a psychiatric hospital much the same as they tried in Providence, Rhode Island and Miami, Florida at Thanksgiving and Christmas but if the Orono, Maine police department was capable of following up on an investigation they would have turned up a past history of abuse perpetrated by my family. The Orono Maine police department is incapable and incompetent of properly protecting the rights of their constituents against fraud and abuse of power by the commanding officer of the Orono, Maine police department.

The Orono, Maine Police Department can also if capable of a thorough investigation would further see evidence of a historical pattern of abuse of the law by the Crandall family and the Orono, Maine police department by their continued ongoing harassment every so often by bothering me

with useless allegations against fraudulent speculation from people who don't even live in the State of Maine.

The Orono police department based on a psychiatric meltdown due to Penobscot Community Health and Counseling withholding for 3 weeks my psychiatric medications creating an intense situation now feels like they can justify breaking the law by performing warrantless searches and illegal Fourth Amendment rights violating strip searches without probable cause.

The Orono, Maine police department is incapable of stopping the continuing ongoing harassment because of the abuse of power by the authority of the chief of police acting in violation of a person's civil rights.

I filed a $160 million dollar lawsuit against the Orono, Maine police department and the Town of Orono Maine mainly in the attempt to get the lawbreakers to back off and leave me and Alice Kate Crandall alone.

William John Crandall, I lived in North Stonington Connecticut until I was 18 years old. I graduated high school from Ella Grasso Southeastern Technical High School in 1988 when I moved to Laramie, Wyoming to attend Heavy Equipment Technician School. I spent a year and a half on my friend Patrick Whitman ranch learning all I could about horses and pro-roping. I returned to the state of Maine after my Wyoming graduation to establish my own horse farm in Lincoln, Maine named Isfappaloosa Farms because I raised show Appaloosas. I unfortunately met with ill health requiring 13 back surgeries 2 of them total fusions to my spine. I took Civil and Environmental Engineering courses while undergoing surgery's and I graduated with a 4.0 GPA. I now reside in Orono, Maine with my wife Alice Kate Crandall. I am working towards my Master Degree in Business Administration and Management at Southern New Hampshire University while I continue to write my children's books.